The Big Apple Turns Brown When You Slice It

Selected Poems and Short Stories of My Nuyorican Culture

By

Jenny Terrero Rivera

Edited by: Berta Radaloff with the help of
Theresa Pagano and "The Westside Learning Center"
in Syracuse N.Y

This book is a work of fiction. Places, events, and situations in this story are purely fictional. Any resemblance to actual persons, living or dead, is coincidental.

ISBN: 1-4033-1126-9 (E-book)
ISBN: 1-4033-1127-7 (Paperback)

Library of Congress Control Number: 2002105697

This book is printed on acid free paper.

Printed in the United States of America
Bloomington, IN

Cover design, Carl Conners
224 Millen Dr. N. Syracuse N.Y 13212

1stBooks - rev. 06/28/02

Dedications:

Dedicated to the following:

SANDRA LOPEZ CLARK, (COOKIE) .my best friend and
sister, for teaching me how to laugh
ISABEL RINCON RIVERA .my mother who sings like a
bird
JULIO RIVERA .my father a poet and designer of awesome
kites

MY BLESSED CHILDREN:
JOHNNY, singer, song writer, musician
ANGELO .singer, song writer, musician
JENNYLOU .poet, artist, sculptor
DAVID .singer, song writer, musician, poet, artist, sculptor

My Latino people and culture, which I believed I had lost,
only to discover that deep inside was a well of Salsa ready
to spring forth.

A SPECIAL THANKS TO:

Jackie Warren Moore, Poet .who encourage me to write
about the culture I believed I had lost.

Bethsida Gonzales .Commissioner of Education .who
encouraged me to continue my education

Brono Putzler .professor of English Literature at Colombia
College .who praised my writing .and gave me only A's

Table of Contents

THE BIG APPLE 1
I AM A BROWN PERSON 2
UNIDAD! 4
MI GENTE 5
EL NEGRO PACHUCO 7
LAS BORICUAS 8
THE MELTING SCAM 10
¡MENTIRA! 11
THE LADY ON THE WATER 13
IN SEARCH OF A PASTEL 15
OUR LATIN SOUND 17
NEWS BULLETIN 19
MAMA 21
¡BASTA YA! GALLO 23
A NUYORICAN I BE 25
SHADES OF BLACK 27
THE AMERICAN BEAUTIFUL WOMAN 28
MY NAME IS 29
PLASTIC SLIP COVERS MADE 31
TO ORDER 31
MESTIZO 33
LET'S DRINK TO THAT 34
BLACK SISTERS—BROWN 35
LA MANZANA 36
PROCESS OF ELIMINATION 38
THE CHOSEN ONE 39
PRISONER OF MY BROTHER 41
DON GUILLERMO 43
P.A. AND ME 49
TO BE LATINA 54
SISTERS IN RECOVERY 56
LOS ALELUYAS 57

GRINGA YOU BE 62
ODE TO JUANA PEÑA 63
SQUATTERS 64
UNDER MY PUERTO RICAN SUN 65
SUBWAY TO MANHATTAN 67
MI FAMILIA 69
OPRAH—IS THE MAN 70
FREDDIE PRINZE 71
CAFE CON GALLETA 72
LA SISTEMA 73
EL ALCOHOL 74
DESPAIR 75
HERITAGE 76
CHOCOLATE MAN 77
NEW YORK -A HELL OF A TOWN 78
MY MOTHER'S PILON 79
PIRAGUA MAN 81
A TRIBUTE TO MY HOME TOWN NEW YORK CITY 82
INFINITE JUSTICE 83
RESURRECTED 84
I WANT TO KNOW WHY 85

THE BIG APPLE

¿Qué es ésto?

No melting pot here, you know
the big apple has been
sliced and diced.

With Little Italy
Chinatown
Harlem
The Village
El Barrio
Broadway
and our ever-existing
Ghetto

territories claimed
and named - defended
to the death.

there be no melting pot
in this New York City town
The BIG APPLE turns brown
when you slice it!

line 1- What is this?

Jenny Terrero Rivera

I AM A BROWN PERSON

I am brown,
though in my veins flow
black and white blood—
African, French, Indian, Spanish.
my colors, mixed well,
mestizo brown; a mixture

I could pretend to be white
if I wanted…If it were necessary
in order to prosper like others do.
I could, after all, I am a Nuyorican.
born of Puerto Rican parents,
raised in the slums of the greatest
city in the world!

I eat my rice and beans while reading
Shakespeare, and lay my head to rest
on a pillow with a beautiful picture of
La Isla del Encanto—the land of happiness
As I listen to the power-filled emotional classics
of my man Mozart.

I speak a Nuyorican Spanish, I dare
not speak in P.R., and live on the
outskirts of the city among white neighbors.
I visit the west side of the city during
Spanish festivals or when I need to
purchase a Spanish product.

Some people say I've sold out:
I am a white person wanna-be.
So! I love my Maxwell House
coffee with my Pastelillo meat pie

Bola de Queso - ball of cheese
I am a brown person
so brown let me be!

Jenny Terrero Rivera

UNIDAD!

No unity! No unity
¡Porqué no hay unidad
entre mi gente!

Flores de millones,
diferentes colores.
Yet we do not grow
upon the same deep
dark rich soil.

Nor do we drink from the
same clear clean waters
that fall from our
full flowing clouds.

¡Porqué no hay unidad
entre mi gente!
Se conocen bien
pero ni se quieren.

We could be the biggest
of peoples - lo más
poderoso de la gente
¡si hubiera UNIDAD!

lines 2&3 why is there no unity among my people
lines 4&5 - millions of flowers of different color
lines 15&16- they know each other well but won't love each other
lines 18&19- we would be a powerful people if there was unity

MI GENTE

Mi gente, mi pueblo - My people, my town
vive en pobreza - live in poverty
los niños andan - the children walk
sin zapatos - without shoes
en una tierra de libertad - in the land of liberty

no hay sueños ni esperanzas - no dreams, no hope
sólo la muerte y la vida eternal - only death and eternal life
la juventud - desanimada - the youth are depressed

ojos sin luz - eyes without light
manos sin libros - hands without books
oídos sin música - ears without music
boca sin voz - mouths without voices
destino sin camino - destiny with no road
corazón sin sentido - hearts without feelings

mi gente, mi pueblo - my people, my town
vive en pobreza - live in poverty
los niños andan sin zapatos - the children walk without shoes
en una tierra de libertad! - in the land of liberty!

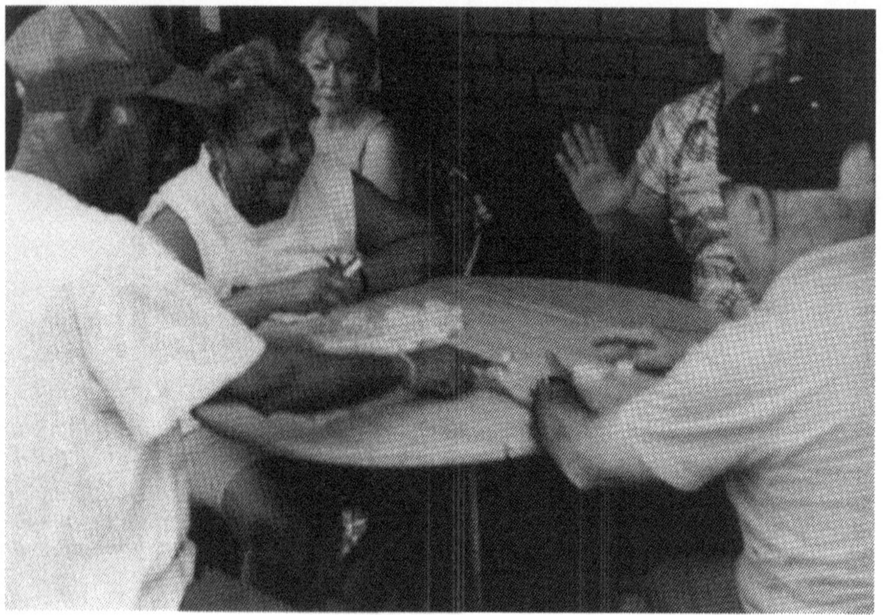

EL NEGRO PACHUCO

El negro Pachuco ¿quién juega con él?
Colt 45 and black-and-white ivory dominoes
rattling beneath the dark-brown worn
wrinkled hands of el negro.

Dueño de una finca en su pueblo Cabo Rojo
pero, he lost it all - his land - con sus bebidas
favoritas, Ron y Whisky y sus mujeres
que bailan Bolero muy close y Merengue
con sabor y ritmo.

Lost his family, lost his home.
now he sits on the corner of Belmont
and Pitken Avenue asking the same thing,
¿Quién juega con Pachuco? ¡Vamos a jugar!
¡El negro Pachuco no quiere pensar!

line-1-who will play with black Pachuco line-6-he use to own some land in Caborojo
line-7-but -with drinking line-8-favorite- rum & whisky and women
line-9-who dance the Bolero really close-slow dancing & Merengue-fast dancing
line-10-with flavor & rhythm lines-14&15-who plays with -lets play
lines-16- black Pachuco does not want to think

LAS BORICUAS

Las Boricuas Latinas bailan
dance your Salsa
dance your Merengue
dance your history
of conquest and survival.

Las Boricuas Latinas bailan
debajo de las Palmas
en sus colores brillantes
against the clear white sand.

In broad flowing skirts
filled with freedom and life,
singing loud. Música de mi
proud people
lifting up the sorrow soul
from depths of despair.

Let the Congas rap and the
Trumpets scream;
Timbales, get out of control.
Ivory keys chime along.

Cantan una canción Latina
de la Isla del Encanto.
Cantamos con el Coquí
my people, humble people,
happy people, make your
sound loud!

Bailan ¡oh! chicas,
no dejen de bailar.
Cantan las historias de

mi gente - no callan
mas!

line-1- the Latin girls dance line-7- underneath the Palm trees line-8- in their bright colors
lines-20 & 21- with a latin song of the Island of joy line-23-sing with the Coqui (tiny frogs)
lines-27&28-dance girls & don't stop line-29&30-sing the history of our people-no more
silence

Jenny Terrero Rivera

THE MELTING SCAM

get your BA, M.S.W., Ph.D..
get it right
wipe out your accent
whatever it be.

the melting pot is boiling, boiling
the melting pot is boiling us away
trying to churn many worlds into one
as many of us die!

speak English! speak English!
to defend yourself,
to make money - to prosper
and grow.

speak it, speak it well
honor the man - obey his commands
stay in your place - don't climb up his
ladder or run in his race!

a token here, a token there
that's the way it's meant to be.
cross the white line, you'll fall on
your knees no matter your

BA, M.S.W. or Ph.D.;
That's America!

¡MENTIRA!

who am I?
¿quién soy? ¿quién soy? who am I
black, brown, red, white
those people-what people
greasy people-lazy people
loud people-esa gente those people
qué gente, mi gente. what people, my people

wilfredo's coming
¡viene wilfredo!
look out for the mail
that time of the month
mi cheque: dinero my check, my money
to dance, drink, and drug;
tiempo de olvidar.
time to forget.

kept in my place
just no escape.
jobs pay too little
checks come too late.
¡estoy cansado ya! I am so tired
I am so tired
me voy a levantar I shall arise
up off my booty - up off my junk

get out of my way!
doors I will, con fuerza, with strength
force open. voy a entrar. I will enter
I will walk through Adelante! Oh, alma muerta.
forward, dead soul
¡Adelante! Oh, mente forward, mind
¡no duermas más! sleep no more

I am. Yo soy! ¡Yo vivo! I am - I live -
esclavitud ¡no más! a slave no more
no longer a slave!

THE LADY ON THE WATER

Mira, Señora, with your long traje,
su lámpara y su libro de verdad.
llamaste mi nombre my name you call

tentadora de sueños - yes, so many dreams.
promesas tan bellas de oro y paz,
you let me down big; you broke my heart.

alejado de mi tierra
you kept calling my name.
lady Liberty on the water
you drove me insane

en lugar de la verdad you gave me lies
instead of peace you stole my mind
instead of dreams you gave me drugs
to dream the dreams that I dream of.

line-1-look lady in the long dress
line-2-your lamp and your book of truth
line-5-beautiful promises of gold and peace
line-7-far I am from my land

Jenny Terrero Rivera

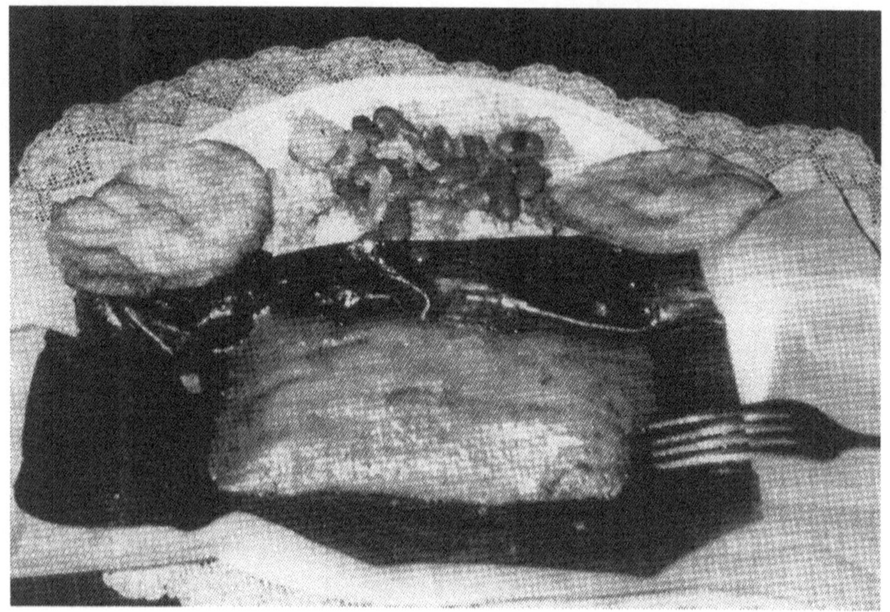

IN SEARCH OF A PASTEL

In this city, in this little city
I search and search on the west side and the south
where my brown people live: ¡Pasteles! ¡Pasteles!
I am looking for Pasteles!
I haven't had one since I moved away from home
Graham Avenue, Brownsville, Brooklyn
loaded with corner restaurants, "La Paloma."
oh, yes, can they cook!

But this town called Syracuse somewhere upstate
nowhere to be found, my Pastel!
can't nobody Latin round here own a restaurant?
man, my mouth waters just thinking about them.
and the first Pastel I found in this hick town
tasted like overcooked plantains hardly stuffed
and yet stuffed with ground meat!
what an insult to a Pastel!

When my mom creates a Pastel, it is a work of art.
she - the Pastel - is wrapped up in hojas de guineos
wrapped again in pastel paper and boiled in salt water
to a juicy steaming golden brown.
when you unwrap her, the tips of your fingers burn
and your mouth waters as her hot steam caresses your
face with and her aroma causes your taste buds to
become anxious for the pleasure she brings.

You discover in her chunks of juicy pernil
seasoned well, chick peas, olives without pits
and a mixture of plátanos, guineos, papas and
calabaza - a Latino masterpiece!
voy para el campo, where my abuelita lives
she will sit me at her table and feed me plate

after delicious Latino plate - I love the way her
house smells - her verduras con bacalao - her
arroz con gandules - but her Pasteles, amigo,

¡VAYA! ARE THE BEST!

OUR LATIN SOUND

vengan los timbales along with
las congas, let them rattle our souls
play la trompeta—fuerte and loud
la Salsa viene de mi black and brown
              gente!

the keys of the piano excite me
oh, alma mía, sing—Oh, espíritu ¡canta!
proud spirit—spirit of my Latino
              sangre!

bailar una Salsa viva - happy música of
my humble people - music de gozo
stories told - passed down de proud 108-
year-old abuelito y abuelita.

¡colores brillantes de my cultura bien
sazonada! Seasoned well with spice,
breathing life - vida into una alma muerta
              live!

breathe gozo en uno desanimado - joy!
breathe healing en un corazón broken!
toca. ¡oh, pueblo mío! canta mi gente
vamos a seguir—adelante—nuestra
bandera flies with life—a powerful
voice in the mist of God's mighty
              viento!

line-1-bring the timbales(latino drums) line -2-the conga drums

line-3-the trumpet-strong & lound line-4-the Salsa (latin dancing) comes from my-people

line-6-my soul-spirit sing line-8-blood line-9-dance a lively Salsa

line-10-joyful music line-12- grandfather & grandmother

line-13-brillant colors of my culture well seasoned line-16- breath life into a dead soul

line-15&16-joy in someone discourage - broken heart line-17 & 18-play my people -sing

line-19&20- lets contune forward line-21 &22- our flag flies with life - wind.

JESUS
Coming
HAVE
YOU MADE
PREPARATION
TO
JESUS

NEWS BULLETIN

¡Noticias! ¡Noticias! on the South side
and the West - Read it in the news.
la gente de colores se matan, ¡se matan!

heading toward the North and East side.
el hombre blanco ya no tiene que hacer nada!

people of color, brown hand or black
killing each other - se matan, for the
colombian man's crack, bought and sold
by the white man's traps.

money for some people of color
to meet their needs, death for other
people of color, victims of disease.

too young to die - let us grow old,
the people of color - led by the nose
follow the smells of drugs that are sold.

falling into traps that keep us down,
turn on each other black, red and brown.
shed our own blood, hate one another,
the people of color — the people of color.

¡qué pena!, ¡que triste es la verdad!
ya no podemos echar la culpa al hombre
blanco - ¡no más! can't blame the white
man's color - no more!

¡Basta ya, la muerte de color!

line-1- news line-3-the people of color are killing themslves

Jenny Terrero Rivera

line-5- the white man no longer has to do it
line-19- how sad is the truth line-21-we can no longer blame the white man
line-23- enough of the death of color

MAMA

No llores más, Mamá
pues sus ojos son para vida y gozo
y no dolor.

* don't cry mamie
someday we'll get
out of the ghetto! *

en sus ojos yo encuentro fuerza y amor
amor que llena mi corazón
fuerza que calma mi alma.
¡adelante! sin cesar ¡no desmayar!

* someday we'll have food
in our cabinet
and meat every day! *

no llores Mamá
flores no lloran
estrellas no dejan de brillar
el Sol nunca se enfría.
tus ojos Mamá, son para vida

don't cry Mamá
flowers don't cry
stars never cease to shine
the sun never grows cold
your eyes Mamá are for life
Vida!

line-1- don't cry anymore mom line-2- your eyes are for life and joy
line-3-and not for pain line-7- in your eyes I find strenth and love
line-8-love that fills my heart line -9-strengh that calms my soul
line-10- forward without ceasing do not faint line14- do not cry mom

Jenny Terrero Rivera

line-15-flowers do not cry line-16-stars do not ceas to shine
line-17-the sun never grows cold line-18- your eyes mom are for life
line-19-don't cry mom line-23-life

¡BASTA YA! GALLO

¿Por qué, oh Gallo, why rooster
do you crow so high and loud?
en la early morning horas.
¡cállate!, oh, Gallo, deja de cantar
shut up,stop singing

why? oh Rooster dude with your
red hood and careful stride
must you sing your mensaje message
so many, mucho times
¡cállate! oh, Gallo, deja de cantar

It's like you're trying to levanter, get up
los que duermen among the dead
those that sleep no want to despertar, wake up
¡cállate! Oh, Gallo, deja de cantar

You start at five a.m.
Y a las ocho I still hear
your at eight sound and feel your mighty
presence making final rounds
¡cállate! oh, Gallo, deja de cantar

Ya, ya está bien enough - ok
I hear and I obey
arise and wake to
a blessed sunny day.
I pull open the shades

¡vaya! the bright sun
I listen but no longer hear
your song being sung

Jenny Terrero Rivera

I ask, amigo Gallo
¿Por qué, dejaste de cantar?
why did you stop

A NUYORICAN I BE

Latin sound, Latin sound
Latin all around and upside down
I search for you inside of me
a Nuyorican's destiny.

the beat and rhythm, is it in my blood?
this Salsa is too spicy for me
the language too fast
the voices too rowdy.

and so they gather, they always gather
my father and his brothers, pulling out
the guitarra, maracas, güiro and congas
and off they go trying to sound hip.
Daniel Santos escapes from my uncle's lips,
Papi sings along to Willie Colón and Mamie
waits to do her impression of La Lupe.

on Avenue D, off the Triboro Bridge
stands a prison made of bricks, it's
metal stairs leading up to the16th floor or more.
my people walked on green pastures
surrounded by multicolored flowers, laughing
as they fed their cows, chickens and pigs.
now they stare at brick walls and climb up
steel mountains

they dwell in a box, no Sun, no Moon,
no black skies filled with big bright shining Stars.
In a stuffy crowded box, they sweat in despair
remembering the hopes and dreams that called them
there
that tall and mighty woman standing on the ocean

floor promised them a new life; so they sit, work,
hope, wait. Tears mix with sweat in a stuffy crowded
box; not home, just the projects!

line-11- guitar-maracas-guiro-an instrument you scrape-drums
line-13- famouse Latin singers

SHADES OF BLACK

Oh my black beauty
tight and muscular - your body close to mine
your black eyes pierce my soul
your plump bright cherry lips press hard upon mine
your lumber-jack arms and hands so smooth
your touch makes me trembling
your small round cute buttocks sit upon the legs
of a mighty antelope - graceful is your leap.

you are my black beauty
Mama won't let me marry you
she says my children would be so black
that I would lose them in the dark
their hair would be coarse,
kinky, difficult, and their blackness
would become their enemy, she'd say

my black beauty, my black pearl, my black ebony
my skin is fair, oh why is my skin fair?
people can't distinguish and my own kind rejects me
noses turned up

shall I take hold of black paint and cover myself?
shall I take black ash and spread it upon my skin?
shall I stand in a fire and let myself burn black?
oh my black beauty forgive my family
for destroying our dream of true love
may I marry a fine-skinned man and our children be
as the eight ball in the side pocket.

ha! ha! my black beauty
you shall remain the color of my eyes
let us run together - let us escape the mixture of colors
let us lay upon the green grass - make love beneath
the bright white stars within a deep black sky!

Jenny Terrero Rivera

THE AMERICAN BEAUTIFUL WOMAN

She is one to catch the eye of both male and female
she turns heads as she gracefully walks by

Frosty snow-white skin without spot or blemish
hugs her wonderful bone structure

Her eyes are alive, the brightest of blue
luscious long lashes that definitely call to you

Her lips are full with passion and lust
Her arms tender, her hands soft to the touch

Her body slender and tall - her breasts not too large
never too small - perfect - full - touchable

Her hips round, her long legs beautiful
and her hair full, flowing, soft, silky, shiny
beneath the sun—and, of course, blond?

I DON'T THINK SO!

MY NAME IS

My name, mi nombre is Ricardo, not Ricky
My nombre, my name is José, not Joe
My name, mi nombre is María, not Mary

Don't take my nombre, don't change my name
I am me—who I am, I am—I claim my claim

I may be poor but I'm ready to work
I may have an accent but I do speak

I may not know much but I'm
willing and ready to learn
I may not have skills but
I'm gifted and talented

Don't say I can't change
when I am ready to turn
Don't put me on the shelf
or label me unlearned

I am who I am and willing to be
My name is Edwaldo, not Ed,
Waldo or Eddie!

Jenny Terrero Rivera

PLASTIC SLIP COVERS MADE
TO ORDER

For one thing, there is plastic
they stick to your skin in the summer
when it's hot and muggy and you're in
your shorts. In the winter the plastic gets
hard and cold releasing air every time you
sit down making everyone think you just
passed gas. God forbid you fall asleep with
your face pressed up against it!

They are noisy and uncomfortable, however
they do keep your furniture clean and looking new.
My father was a smart man, he knew poor people
couldn't afford two sets of furniture in one life time.
So, being the entrepreneur that he was, he set out
with his used black Singer Sewing Machine, his wife
and four young children to the land of opportunity:
AMERICA!

With the help of P.A. he set up shop in a tiny
corner storefront on the lower east side of
Brooklyn;

"JULIO'S PLASTIC SLIP COVERS"
MADE TO ORDER

You could get them in 12 gauge plastic or 16 gauge
plastic, 16 being of the better quality. You had a choice
of clear plastic or gray blue with gold or silver trimming
along with a one-year warranty, even if it did turned yellow.
He was such a creative man and carried his ability to the
extreme, becoming possessed by the plastic - it taking

total control of his every waking hour.

He would drag us kids along on his long life-threatening
journey through Manhattan's Delancy Street, where
yellow monsters - and riders on two wheels competed
for the black tar - dodging the yellow wild beast.
Surviving the terrors of the city we nervously arrived at
the mysterious smelly and gloomy warehouse becoming
sick as we found ourselves hopelessly surrounded by hundreds
of gigantic roles of plastic

My fathers dealer would silently creep out from behind one of
the many dusty isles - his black thick frame glasses hanging on
the tip of his big nose. He'd mumble the familiar greeting only
pop could understand while puffing on a nasty smelly piece of
cigar that hung from his lips. He was a small skinny little old
man wearing baggy black paints, a black vest, a white long
sleeve shirt with a black tie pulled loose and on top of his bald
head sat a funny little round black cap.

After the usual money exchange pop would have us kids
haul huge roll after huge plastic roll into his station wagon.
He began to make plastic covers for everything he convinced
himself needed a cover. Lamp shades, dining tables and chairs,
car seats, washing machines, books, photo albums, and,
finally, toasters!

YES, I SAID TOASTERS!

And thus he did achieve the AMERICAN DREAM!
He is now retired and lives from his savings in a big
beautiful house he designed and built himself in:

CASA BLANCA LUQUILLO, P.R.

MESTIZO

No! no! we come in all different colors
Latin people live all around the world - fool!
No! no! not all Spanish speaking people
are Puerto Ricans

And guess what? Some of us have blonde
hair and blue eyes. WOW! Ain't that a trip
Bet you never would have believed that one

Remember bro, we are a mixed people
BLACK-WHITE-RED AND BROWN

MESTIZO!

Jenny Terrero Rivera

LET'S DRINK TO THAT

¡VAMOS! Let's pitch in
compramos una botella de Ron,
Johnny Walker Red, Old English 800,
a pint of Bacardi Light,
whatever our pennies afford.

Let's just pitch in so we can get high
forget the man and his ungodly plans
to make us all white!

¡VAMOS! let's get together and speak
our language—help me to remember
before I forget, the Spanish I speak
is not even the best.

In P.R. they laugh
in New York they joke
my language is fading
soon to be lost.

HABLA Español
rebel to his plan
don't melt
don't burn
jump out if you can!

PASAME LA BOTELLA, BRO pass me the bottle
LETS DRINK TO THAT!

BLACK SISTERS—BROWN

Wrapped in my black skin
living in a white city among my
light-skinned sisters denying the
black beneath their light skin, brown;

Passing off as white — for what?
To survive: make it — a better job
a better position, respect!

To be part of the so-called
superior race, they say.
Hey, don't hide, don't play
don't deny and live a lie.

And they, my sisters turn their
light-skinned noses up at little
black me and pretend they are
different — better — but ha! ha!

Their blackness runs deep within
their black veins giving birth to the
black children they don't wish to see
black-skinned children just like me!

Jenny Terrero Rivera

LA MANZANA

Watch your back compay there be no
brotherhood in the streets of The Apple
Delancy street swarms with mixture,
who's who behind slanted eyes
and my own kind, pendejo no seas!

Confía en nadie, pana,
check out the street vendors
with their twenty-dollar tricks,
gold watches ain't gold
and the girls that seem old
selling their souls
younger than your lustful
eyes could see—the little
niña under thirteen.

Vaya brother, vamos a velar
la gente de colores kiss the
man's behind as he robs him blind
under Time Square lights and
Broadway.

Selling dreams-lying machines
oiga mi hermano there be no
American dream!

Take what you can—lie—cheat
and scam, while they jog through
Central Park West-con su shorts
y su tenis, as I play my Quatro
and sing my Boricua songs.

Toss me a quarter - dáme un dime

Hear me sing coritos of the
man's many lies!

line-1-godfather line-5- don't be a fool line-6-don't trust anybody line-14-young girl
line-15&16-lets go watch the people of color line-21-hear me brother line-25-with their
line-26- tenis shoes - quatro-six string guitar line-28-give me a dime

Jenny Terrero Rivera

PROCESS OF ELIMINATION

Eliminate the red people
with the long black hair,
multicolored feathers
who wear animal skins
and live in tents — painted
faces and ritual dance.

Eliminate the white people
with silky hair and bright blue
eyes — pockets bulging and
jewelry stores filled with golden
crosses and candlesticks, wearing
funny little hats and speaking gibberish.

Eliminate the people who have been
burned by the sun, dark as the night,
who sing the blues and spiritual tunes
proud and strong determined to fight!
Remove - kill - destroy - every trace!

Eliminate those who pray to the
Mother of God with guns in their
hands - Bibles on their laps,
eliminate those born on the wrong
side of the tracks, wipe them all out
anyway you can!

Eliminate all lovers
of the same sex
their love is impure
they all deserve death

we are a people so full of hate
I wonder if GOD made a mistake?

THE CHOSEN ONE

Are all Latin men great lovers?
so they say, so they say
could it be they really are?

so they say, so they say

The Latin man, the Latin Don Juan, Latin lover
says you are his number one woman - you are
the chosen one to bare his children - no other;
you are special - you have won the prize.

so they say, so they say

To you he will come home every night
after he has sucked on Conchita's breast
and smelled Juanita's neck - and spilled his
semen into Yolanda's cave.

so they say, so they say

No matter - he sleeps only in your bed
the chosen one who bore his kids and washes
his clothes, cooks his arroz con pollo y
habichuelas rosadas, aguacate y ensalada.

You lay your head on his machismo chest
and get to carry his name - after all
he is your latino man, your latin Romeo.

so they say, so they say.

Jenny Terrero Rivera

PRISONER OF MY BROTHER

Yo, Moon Baby, ¿Qué es esto?
What you do to your blood, man?
En nuestras calles — on our streets
in our neighborhood, on every corner
en cada esquina bro — they softly scream
out loud — nos llaman and are seen
for miles around — los veo, forcing our
people to pull out their green to medicate
the pain, ease the disease ¿Qué es esto?
Handing out freebees

(Prisionero de mi hermano) prisoner of my brother

Spic of Spics
lower than the roaches
that crawl on my stove
Slicker than the rats
that bite at my toes as I try to sleep
in an old abandoned crack house
no cama for me — I lay in my disease no bed

(Prisionero de mi hermano)

Like the dog you climb on your brothers' back,
tongue hanging out, dripping saliva on a hot
stuffy day behind our neighborhood bodega spanish grocery
"MI FAMILIA," where we used to get credit
to feed our families — no credit now
In the alley we pay you for no more pain

(Prisionero de mi hermano)

You won't climb off till we stick to you

so hooked and sick we cannot move
we hurt too much — nothing left to lose
Pana — amigo — hermano friend,brother
no eres tu — no friend of mine
not my brother — no, not you.

DON GUILLERMO

Don Guillermo, smooth were his strong hands over those white ivory dominoes. As a child I hovered over his shoulders tickled by the rattling sounds of the dominoes, trying not to choke on the smell of the famous Cuban cigars he frequently sucked. He'd fill his tiny thick glass with a clear liquid and tossing his head back, gulp down the strong smelling liquid that seemed to burn his throat every time yet filled him with laughter. He'd gulp down one after another as I watched his moves and the eyes of each player trying their best to beat the best.

Don Guillermo was serious about his game, often betting twenty-and fifty-dollar bills. I longed to be just like him, tossing money around like he had no need for it. I often wondered how he made all that money. He'd just hang around all day playing dominoes. I came to conclude that playing dominoes and betting must be the way he makes money. So I decided to learn all I could about the game every time he played.

Roughly between six drinks and nearing towards the end of the game, something always occured to tick Guillermo off sending him into a frenzy. Some dispute, not always about the game but over casual conversations. Like who was more important, the virgin Mary or Jesus Christ. Guillermo loved to debate as if he knew the true answer to every question. He would go on and on with "How can they call a mere women the mother of God? as if God could have or even needed a mother."

Sometimes things would get so heated that Don Guillermo would tip the playing table over, run into his garage and get his old beat-up history-filled machete. He would storm out of his garage an absolutely crazed man, with intoxicated demons in his blood, chasing down his perceived enemy shouting, "Hijo de gran puta! Te colto la cabeza!"

I knew he was cursing but I never really knew what those words meant.

My heart would pump hard and fast with excitement, hoping to see blood and wondering if he would ever really cut someone's head off. It being quite possible, and not the first time this side of El Barrio. In P.R. there were many a tale about people that fell victims of lost and mangled limbs, but here in the Barrio it would be a first for Don Guillermo.

4th para-line 4- son of a bitch I'll cut your head off

I'd laugh and laugh watching his old greasy, flabby, pot-bellied self, galloping after his prey like an old wasted dizzy bear his first day out of hibernation. Oh, how Don Guillermo loved reliving those good-old hot-blooded Puerto Rican days. Everyone knew he always hoped someone would tick him off or challenge him just so he could have an opportunity to play with his machete.

People humored him, and after his fill of adventure he would sit under the shade of our favorite old oak tree and begin his many wonderful and exciting tales. I loved everyone of them.

I remember the tale he told about a dispute between Jaime and Moreno (Moreno's real name was Marcos). That story sent chills up and down my twelve-year-old spine. Especially the way Don Guillermo acted out scene after every exaggerated scene. As the story goes, Marcos hated when people called him Moreno— Moreno means black person. Marcos would argue that he isn't black (even if his skin is so black that it's blue,) because he is Puerto Rican, and not a black American.

Jaime would tease him, saying he wasn't in Puerto Rico. He was now in America—New York—and viewed as a black American, in short, Moreno. "Mira carajo! ¡Coño!" Moreno would scream out. "No me llames prieto porque te mato, oiga!" Guillermo said the veins in Moreno's neck would pop thick as he would get all up in Jaime's face. Jaime would just laugh and continue with his teasing, "ay, tan sensitivo—si eres negro! Eres negro condenado! Ni tu madre que te dio vida te llamará otro nombre aquí en Nueva York sino moreno lindo!" he'd laugh.

Guillermo would begin to laugh, too, reliving the story and stretching out his hand so I could help him stand. Still laughing with his mind in the past, he would begin to search for some matches, interrupting his story, licking his lips and reaching into his shirt pocket for one of his Cubans.

I would stare and wait in anticipation wishing he would find his matches and get on with the story, feeling like I was being teased by his time-consuming method of lighting up his Cuban. First he'd pull it out of the pack, then he would bring it horizontally up to his nose and sniff it deeply, as if he were smelling the fragrance of an exotic flower. "Now dat is a good cigar," he'd say to me as though revealing some vital information for my future success. Then he'd bring it under my nose and command me to sniff. "Sniff, I say, muchacho, take a deep sniff."

para-9-line-3- do not call me black - I will kill you - you hear me-
line-5 & 6- oh so sensitive, but you are black - dam you - not even your mother that gave you life would call you by any other name here in New York, than pretty black boy

I'd smell the darn thing and dread what I knew was coming next. Finally he'd find his matches, bite off the tip of the cigar and, spitting it out, look at his unlit Cuban as though it were being prepared to be offered to the gods. He would light it and begin puffing away, blowing the smoke into the air. He'd lick his lips with delight, taking deep drags.

Then he would push it into my mouth and say, with his funny broken English, "Now yu go, take smoke like an hombre." I would choke and cough and he would just break out laughing, "Ha! Ha! some day yu kil fo a cuban." He'd slump back down under the tree and continue the story, which was worth the one or two minutes of being tormented by inhaling the smoke of a Cuban cigar.

"Moreno, I mean Marcos, got so fed up with Jaime's, that he got quite an he turn an leave
but Moreno, he com back later da day." Guillermo whispers slowing the pace of the story and getting close to my face, he looks me in the eye and in a mysterious tone says, "Day was all looking at Isabel's car. Isabel was Jaime's mujer an Jaime's broda was der and Jaime's broda's frien was der too day all looking at de car, car no wan to work."

"Wen all de sading who come lik a toro out of no place looking lik he want de matador, but Moreno—I mean Marcos," he chuckles taking a deep drag of his cigar. "Marcos, com wit de shot gun, escreaming, like una mujer loca. Coño! Ahora termino contigo! Jaime, he girlfriend an he broda frien turn aroun wit day eyes so big, lik dis" Guillermo places his to hands around his eyes and forces his eyes wide open..
Day was ascared to def an day no can move.

"Jaime lik un estupido says, MORENO! estás loco!" Now Marcos is so crazy, he says "Te atreves llamarme Moreno,

pendejo, cuando tengo esta alma!" An he estart shooting like un loco da escap from crazy house. He get Isabel's arm and breast, and he mes up Jaime's broda face and mak big hole in Jaime's stomach yu could see through."
I gasp in excitement.

Guillermo would then take a break to give me time to soak in the scenes. He'd look at his watch, "Now I no why mi stomach is making all dat noise, yu hear dat?" pointing to his stomach, "dat mean it time to comer." He'd motion for me to give him a hand standing up again. I'd grab ahold of his dark wrinkled hand and pull, wanting Guillermo to notice how strong I am.

"Yu getin prety strong muchacho," he'd say proudly as he'd get to his feet. "Vámonos, lets go eat like hombres eh! Yu know what happen to Moreno after he did dat?" "No, what happened? Tell me," I would plead. He was just as anxious to tell as I was to hear.

Guillermo would continue, "Well he go talk to mush, like he som big shot yu kno, after he was pick up by la policía and in jail—he was a stil talking mucho, he say to de other chicos in jail, "das right I am Marcos—das me, no play with me—I blow yu cabeza away! Talk about loco, da he was."

Remember I said before that Guillermo always exaggerated his stories?. Well, the truth was that Marcos did show up with an old shotgun. He fired the thing like a nut case—skinned Jaime's head, nicked Isabel's arm and breast, slightly wounded his brother and his buddy—but before he could reload and continue firing, the moldy-old shotgun, fell apart right in his hands.

Even though Marcos felt humiliated over the shot gun falling apart in his hands, he was also proud of himself. And he did go around the prison warning everyone that he would kill anybody who called him Moreno. Well what can I say? Never warn an imate about what he should not do. Nevertheless, Marcos never did complete his seven month term. I wonder way? I always knew that Guillermo exaggerated his stories but that never bothered me, after all he was so good at making the truth a lot more exciting.

para- 12- line 3 & 4- a crazy woman - now I finish you
para-13- line 1 - stupid- your crazy line 2 - you dare call me a fool when I am armed

P.A. AND ME

It's Monday morning of June the second and I am not enthusiastic about the day ahead. The time for recertification has once again arrived with P.A. (public assistance), in which I must appear for battle and plead my case if I am to continue to receive aid. I get my three children up for school and rush around like a mad woman, trying to get everybody ready.

As they head out the door I quickly gulp down my breakfast—a cup of black coffee—as I reach for the large brown envelope loaded with ammunition and rush out the door to my ten o'clock appointment.

As I step outside, I quickly notice how hot and stuffy it is and dread the thought of having to take two trains through the city battlegrounds. Arriving at the station, I begin to descend into this slimy underground dungeon. My eyes immediately notice the puddles and stains of dry smelly urine that invade my nostrils, making my stomach turn as usual.

Thus begins my careful walk through the minefields; evading the puddles, bums, drunks, nut cases and ever present perverts, who for some unknown reason seem to be drawn to me.

I hate the New York City subway system with a vengeance. I find myself constantly looking over my shoulder for fear that some nut case will push me onto the train tracks. Eventually, I hear the faint rumbling of a train approaching from deep down the dark eerie tunnel and catch a glimpse of its bright white headlights. "Well, it's about time," I grumble, as the train roars by, offering me a fast-forward view of multicolored faces.

The doors slither open like a snake ready to swallow its pray. I rush over to a clean available seat by the window. I settle myself and begin to stare at all the advertisements and graffiti sprawled over the walls, windows, doors, chairs and ceiling—disgusting.

My comfortable ride begins with a loud roar of the train and the gut—twisting screeching of its iron wheels, the opening and closing of doors, being jerked back and forth, lights flashing on and off—they all make me dreadfully paranoid. In my car there are poor, middle class and old people children crying; and loud obnoxious teen-agers cutting class, smoking, laughing and picking on helpless people filled with fear.

A bum takes up three seats sleeping peaceably, while a Muslim dude goes from car to car selling incense and preaching some hype about Elija Mohammed, running right into his competition in our car.
He stares angrily down at this long-haired, bushy-bearded, wasted Vietnam veteran in his wheelchair, begging for handouts, still wearing his army fatigues and resembling Bob Dylan. I drop a quarter into his can.

Finally, I reach my destination, Liberty Avenue, feeling relieved that the office is in my borough and not in Manhattan. As I go through the turnstile and walk up the steps to the streets, I am nearly knocked over by a group of black youths running away from who knows what.

Once at the top of the steps, the heat of the sun burns deep into my skull, as hot, thick air pollutes my lungs. Immediately, this scummy, tall skinny Puerto Rican dude stops me, "Hey Babe, want to buy a beautiful watch for your man?" His nasty breath hits me with full force and I wonder how I will survive this encounter.

"Just ten dollars," he continues, as I try to get around him while shaking my head no, but he steps right in front of me with his long-sleeve flannel shirt (to cover his tracks no doubt), and a face dripping sweat. His hands are shaking and he is talking fast as he stubbornly shoves the watch in my face, demanding that I look it over.

This guy obviously needs his fix so I'd better be nice to him. "Oh, yeah bro, it's a nice watch and if I had ten dollars I would buy it, but hey, no dinero, sorry."
He turns away from me as quickly as he arrived and wastes no time spotting his next potential customer. I rush off, dodging all other street-corner entrepreneurs, but cannot help but notice this white women about twenty-five walking painfully slow. I knew immediately that she was stoned out of her mind.

Wasted, she is nodding on her feet. She takes a few steps, then stops and stands still, slowly bending over at the waist as though the sun was literally melting her. When she is about to tumble over, she straightens up again, takes a few steps, stops, and begins to bend over again.

I watch her awhile to see if she will hit the floor, but she never does. Once I arrive at the P.A. building I have to use one of the ten phones lined up at the back wall. The phones were for clients to call their workers to inform them of their arrival. Then, I go to a large waiting area, take one of the many seats and wait an hour or two or three or four, waiting for my worker to call my name.

The place is crowded; the security guards are fat; the bathrooms are filthy with clogged—up toilets and overflowing garbage cans. There are so many people needing help, some loud and nasty, others quiet and patient. The majority of the people are black and Hispanic, a few are white. There are mothers with several children, entire families, and many addicts and alcoholics.

I deliberately dress down to fit the role correctly. Some clients, mainly black and Hispanic actually come in all fancied up, wearing leather jackets, patent-leather shoes or new expensive name-brand sneakers, gold earrings, necklaces and chains, which only makes the worker believe that they are milking the system. (which a few of all races do)

I am so hungry that my stomach has declared war—rumbling and grumbling to get my attention. I know I'd better respond soon to the soldiers in my belly before they take out their bayonets and begin stabbing my stomach with pain. Some Hispanic kids are running around while their mother is threatening them shouting in Spanish, "I am going to break your face if you don't come sit down!"

Suddenly there is a scuffle by the intake windows. A black mother of two is shouting, demanding to see her worker. "I want my money, damn it!` I want my money! You call my worker, that bitch! She closed my case! You people lost my papers, not me! I demand to speak to her supervisor!" She is asked to calm down several times which she is unable to do. So they call the security guards and have her tossed out.

I wonder how some people have the nerve to demand anything. I have been waiting three hours now and I am really feeling nauseous, so I decide to ask the lady next to me if she could listen for my name while I run to the grocery store across the street. She agrees.

Shortly after my return, my worker calls my name. I jump to my feet with a tight grip on my brown envelope filled with ammunition, and follow her big butt to a long narrow section of office tables. She is heavy, black, well-dressed—with a two-piece suit, and high heeled shoes—and obviously on a power trip (for sure an oreo cookie).

As we reach her designated office space, she ever-so-gracefully sits upon her meticulous and majestic throne and, with her long bright-blood-red claws for fingernails, reaches for her only needed weapon: her pen. "Do you have ALL your documents?" She is cold, rude, and hates the fact that she must work eight hours a day while I, in her opinion, sit on my butt at home, eating, sleeping, drinking and waiting for my check.

I hate her. She does not possess any of the good qualities that my last worker had. In response to her question, I reach for my weapon, the brown envelope, and proceed to pull out birth certificates, Social Security cards, current school letters, landlord letter, rent receipt for the last six months, electric, gas and phone bills; Medicaid cards and current medical reports. My heart is pounding as I watch her slowly examine every document. I am breaking out in a sweat as she pauses, and I wonder if I forgot something. She looks deviously for any error on my part, any document I may have overlooked, any reason whatsoever to close my case; like a judge hammering down with his mallet she eagerly wants to exercise her power over me and with her mighty pen write the words, "Case Closed." Frustrated in her search, she gives up and goes off to make her copies.

She takes her time, chats with co-workers a while. stops to get a cup of coffee and in slow motion heads back. She squeezes her big butt into her throne and opens her mouth like a snake about to strike, "It seems you have everything in order."

She sets up my next appointment and lets me go. Triumphantly I stand to my feet, proudly take hold of my brown envelope and walk out the doors to face the mine-fields of the four O'clock rush hour. All this for a lousy check and food stamps that barely meets my families needs. GOD BLESS AMERICA!

Jenny Terrero Rivera

TO BE LATINA

You my friend will sense my obvious fear and resistance in having to take part in the opening of spiritual doorways. They will lift up the heavy thick veil which has been woven in inherited darkness passed on through the ages. Magic spells and curses practiced by las brujas, las hijas de Don Pubido, el Santero del barrio de Vieques.

The witches are the daughters of Don Pubido, the sorcerer of the small town of Vieques in Puerto Rico. Tales are told over and over as though there was some immortal glory locked away in the words. Don Pubido is a short, dark-skinned, greasy-looking, overweight Puerto Rican slob of a man. If you stand next to him, you note the odor of a dead beast emanating from his being.

His eyes are as black as coal. When he looks at you, his eyes seem to pierce your soul as he reveals to you secrets you have shared with no one. He begins his mysterious melodic chant and ritual dance: a hypnotic, intoxicating, unbalanced, exaggerated dance. He pulls from his person multicolored strips of material, each about a yard in length.

He dances around the room as though lead by these strips. He caresses everyone in the room with them, as if the strips had some sort of repellent that would rid the person of evil.

He is groaning in some other language that I can't understand. Don Pubido becomes aggressive in his chanting. He takes out a cigar, lights it, and places the lit side into his mouth, takes out the cigar and blows the smoke into my face, commanding me to breathe it in. He is called a white witch, "Brujo blanco, bueno es, el doctor de los vecinos." He is the neighborhood doctor. When his medicine fails to work he attributes it to the will of God.

Mama calls on him from time to time. Today he will cast out the spirit of Jezebel. The neighbors have convinced Mama that I am a chaser of men. I have yet to sleep with anyone. I am branded the black sheep who has deviated from the straight and narrow. My convergence shall be a transcending victory for el brujo, el Santero, el doctor de los ignorantes de Vieques.

The doctor of the ignorant villagers of the town of Vieques. Mama would tell me tales about the hands of the dead that would come up from underneath her bed at night to grab her and pull her to their underworld. She always made it her business to make sure that no part of her body hung out of the bed.
They, the witches, have altars in their homes in some dark corner of a room. This altar is occupied by a large statue of Jesus and Mary along with many other saints. Large crosses, rosaries, many candles, fruit bowls and wine glasses always filled with offerings of fruit and drink surround the saints.

Smoke is filling the room now, as women in long white dresses and head scarves join him. He is in the middle, surrounded by these women, as they all chant and hum, making strange sounds. I am really frightened and I want desperately to get out. The air is choking me as one of the women pulls me into the circle. I try to resist but it seems I've lost my strength.

They are going around me in a circle and the room seems to be moving. I feel that I will lose my balance. Something is happening to me. I can't fight it; my arms are numb and my eyes are closed. I am speaking or singing, I cannot tell which. I feel like I am floating, as though I have taken some sort of drug.

I begin to pray, "Lord, God help me—get me out of this," when suddenly everything turns black. When I finally awake I realize that I am lying on the sofa. Everyone is gone and Mama is standing over me, saying something about the ritual being a success. Another triumph for Don Pubido and his crew. Another day in the life of a Latino female Jezebel.

Jenny Terrero Rivera

SISTERS IN RECOVERY

Mira, Sara, slow down my little
four-foot Rosie Perez, Puerto Rican
sound-alike sister with your
Speedy Gonzalez self—
ever since you got clean, baby,
you just up and running

Mira, Sara, suave con paciencia,
one day at a time—don't sweat it
take your time; your higher power
is in control—his divine plan -
to save your soul

Mira, Sara, you're now clean and free
of all your addictions just like me
So let's stay cool and slow down,
smell the roses, look at the moon,
take in a movie, shoot some pool

Hey, little sister, all is OK
that's what happens when you turn
your will over and finally pray,
one day at a time hermana,
just for today

line-7- be smooth-patient
line-20- sister

LOS ALELUYAS

That Pentecostal church across the street sounds like they are jamming and throwing some kind of party with all the shouting and loud music blasting. "Ale…lu…yaaa!…Gloo…ria Dios!"…the preacher screams out and the people shout back, "Amen!" …"Hermanos, a su nombre!"… again he screams out and the people shout back, "Gloria!" …"uno!..dos!…y tres!" he continues. "Quien vive!" he shrieks at the top of his powerful lungs. "Cristo!" they shout back in unison.

This guy surely knows how to stir up emotions and get a crowd going. Each question he throws out at the congregation causes an accelerated response until the entire church is caught up in a loud frenzy. They are up on their feet shouting and throwing their hands up in the air as though they are at a stadium cheering on the last game of the season."And by God, there goes the number one player on the team with the football. Jesus Christ! He's got the ball! There are only two minutes left to the game… and he's off and running! … The crowd is going crazy cheering him on. Get out of his way! He's flying down the field knocking over his Satanic opponents, slipping through their futile attempts to tackle and bring him down."

"He is the team's only hope for survival. The battle is too great and the team is growing weary. Jesus must get to the gold and save the team from defeat. He is running full speed ahead, the ball tucked underneath his arm. No one can stop him or get in his way! Ladies and gentlemen, he just reached the gold, he's tossing the ball to the ground, lifting his hands up high in victory. He has done it again! What a defeat for the Satanic opponents!"

The crowd is going wild; Jesus has done it again! He never fails!

His teammates, overjoyed, are lifting him up onto their shoulders and parading him around the stadium. The roar of the fans is explosive! They are rushing onto the field. This is what I am imagining as I lay in bed at 8:30 p.m. on a school night and I can't no way sleep because tonight is the second night of a Wednesday, Thursday, Friday and Saturday night, Campana Misionera, which is a four-day missionary campaign at the Pentecostal church right across the street from my bedroom window. A preacher is up from Puerto Rico. They say he is the famous Yeye Avila.

The aleluyas have been going around the neighborhood door to-door since last month, giving out flyers and inviting people to attend. I heard that he used to be the Mr. America of the Latin world until God called him to be a preacher. I had grown anxious to see him and got my first glimpse of him Wednesday night, the first night of the campaign. I didn't think much of him until he opened his mouth and began to preach. He was loud and frightening like a wild animal. He'd press his lips to the mic and scream out to the people, "A..le..lu..yaaa! ...Glo..riaaa.. Dio..sss!"

I had already made plans to sneak out of the house Wednesday night after waiting for Mom to fall into a deep sleep. Once her snoring began I knew she was out cold. It was my only chance to see this ex-Mr. America in action. Mom refused to give me permission to attend one of the services, and if she had caught me sneaking out, she'd have had my butt for sure.

I begged her to let me go but she argued, saying, "Esos locos Pentecostales, oh no, muchacho, no te quiero ver ni cerca de esa iglesia." She doesn't want me anywhere near those crazy people, she'd firmly say. "Están endemoniados," she'd explain that she believes they are possessed by the Devil.

Every time I would question Mom's opinion and belief concerning the Aleluyas, she'd stop me in mid-sentence and rush off to her sanctuary at the corner of her bedroom. My mother, a devout Catholic woman, took my questions seriously to her prayer corner.

Although my mother had difficulty kneeling down because of her weight, once settled, she'd begin by anointing her head with Holy oil. Then she'd take her rosaries into her hands and begin to pray, bringing my rebellious questions to the attention of Saint Mary the mother of God and all those other saints she prayed to.

"Santa Maria, Madre de Dios, no permites que esa gente loca, edemoniada, engañen a mi pobre hijito inocente." She'd pray to the mother of God for me and for my protection from the crazy Pentecostals.

"Pero Mamá," I would argue, "Donna Lucy next door had cancer y los Alelujas oraron por ella and she was healed. They prayed and it was a miracle, Ma." "No, no, hijito ella está engañada." She tells me that Donna Lucy is being deceived into believing that she is healed. "Son demonios." Lying Demons she says. Confused, I ask curiously, "Pero Mamá, I thought demons were supposed to be bad and do bad things to people, not good things." She gets frustrated with me and I decide to let Mom believe what she wants to believe. Anyway, I liked Donna Lucy and was happy that she wasn't sick anymore, whether her miracle was conjured-up by aleluyas or the demons.

I was lying in bed Wednesday night listening to the music blasting and the people shouting as Mr. Ex-America was going wild on the mic. I just had to see what all the excitement was about and why Mama and other people referred to the Pentecostals as crazy people. I was tossing and turning in bed and trying to shut out the noise. I buried my head under my pillow but the sound of the drums, guitars, tambourines and of course Mr. Avila's powerful voice, all came through my bedroom window loud and clear. His intense, deep raspy voice and preaching style was electrifying.

I got out of bed and sat on a chair by the window hoping to see what was going on in the little church across the street. The door of the church was wide open and there were two women in white dresses standing at the entrance handing out programs as they greeted the people arriving. Suddenly I developed an uncontrollable urge to meet Mr. Ex-America and learn for myself what the Aleluyas were all about. And I convinced myself that I just could not pass up the opportunity.

So I impatiently waited for Mom to fall asleep, then nervously tip-toed out of the house and ran fast across the street in anticipation of the excitement ahead. The small storefront church was packed with people, making it easy for me to slip in unnoticed among the people standing at the rear of the church.

I desperately wanted to see what was going on but I couldn't because of all the adults blocking my view. It was hot and people were fanning themselves even though the two old ceiling fans were going full speed. The music was fast and loud and this guy, Yeye, was touching people, praying for them, roaring like an animal into their faces, and talking in some strange weird language. People were falling to the floor.

To get a closer look, I had to push my way through the crowd. Once up close, I thought the preacher looked like a regular man. He was slightly muscular but he wasn't huge or tall and he didn't even look strong. I was disappointed. I had expected to meet an Arnold Schwarzenegger-type preacher.

Anyway, as he prayed for people, some would fall to the floor in a deep sleep. Some people looked like they were dancing. Others shook violently, while still others cried. The service was

fascinating and ended around eleven-thirty that night. The next day I was so tired in the morning that Mom had to call three times to get me out of bed so I could get ready for school. "Eso Alelujas no le jeu sleep hijito?" she asked
while handing me a plate of two hard-boiled eggs and toast. "Dey no le mi sleep con tanta buja," she complained. "Yea, Mom, they were so noisy last night, it took me forever to fall asleep," I agreed, chiming in with her complaints while gulping down my breakfast.

Tonight is the last night of the campaign and I wish I had the nerve to sneak out again but I wouldn't dare take another chance. Mom would beat my butt raw and I would be saying the rosary for days. So I am just lying here in my bed listening to the service, imagining myself as a sports reporter sitting in the sports booth screaming excitedly into the mic, ... "It's Jesus and the Heavenly Disciples in the football finale game of the year against The Satanic Red Devils!"

"Wow! Jesus has the ball and he and his Angels are on a serious mission out there on the field! ... Slamming up against Satan and his Red Devils! ...The Devils have been cheating and breaking the rules... It's been foul after foul! ... Everything they try against Jesus' team fails, ladies and gentlemen! It's Jesus with the ball and he's heading for the gooold! I start drifting in and out of sleep as the roar dies down and the Pentecostal service begins to wind down. I see Jesus heading for the Gold, crossing the line and triumphantly tossing the ball to the ground, as his teammates pick him up onto their shoulders.

I am in the sports booth, my mouth up close to the mic, and like a roaring lion I am shouting..."Yes! ...yes! ... Je...sussssss! ... Chri.....st! It's a slaughter! It's a TKO! The crowd is going wild and rushing out unto the field. Everyone is shouting! A...le....lu...yaaa! Glo...ria Di...oos!" I smile and whisper while drifting off to sleep, "Great game, Jesus—you're soooooo cool."

Jenny Terrero Rivera

GRINGA YOU BE

Yo, where you been?
back in town almost a year now
can't pick up the phone and call
your Latina hermana
now that you're home!

Maybe you're just too busy
with your new professional
masters degree - gringo friends
forgetting your brown skin,
rice with beans and Puerto
Rican Rum - gringa you be!

Sipping your white wine or sparkling
champagne, dancing that hillbilly line junk,
white man's imitation of Salsa
forgetting your Latin beat,
losing your Latin Soul!

What is it with you? White wanna-to-be
banana hick from the old country
So! your back in town, well don't even
call me cause you stop being brown!

ODE TO JUANA PEÑA

Come together and play a ballet,
an ode to Juana Peña, who hacked her man to death.
He was sleeping around with Monchita, a sexy,
Iris Chacon look-alike who made it big
shaking her big butt on nationwide T.V

Monchita mixed up a potion at her storefront
Botanica to entice Juana Peña's man, loving, faithful
husband of ten years, father of three.When Juana found
out, she waited outside Monchita's house. Juana's anger
grew to a hot steaming, boiling, vengeful fire as she hid
behind a tree. Finally Juana's husband comes out, kissing
Monchita good-bye - when from behind the tree leaps
out,
Juana Peña, with machete in hand, screaming
"condenado!
sin verguenza! Te mato!" as she hacks him to pieces.

Monchita looks on, too shocked to move, to stunned to
scream, as Juana Peña turns towards Monchita, swings
the machete, and off comes Monchita's head, rolling on
the ground to a bloody stop. Juana Peña spent the rest of
her life in jail, leaving behind her three children, who live
on the streets, and the immortal legacy of a blood-stained
machete and two grave stones that read; "If you are one
for mixing potions beware! JUANA PEÑA'S potion,
a mix of - vengeance - sharp iron and blood!

line-13 &14- dam you without shame I will kill you

Jenny Terrero Rivera

SQUATTERS

Squatters live on land

they pick and choose,

Build their tiny tin houses and there they dwell

Pay no taxes
pay no rent

no man can rule their lives

for even if the man does try

The Squatters pick up and

move to the other

side.

UNDER MY PUERTO RICAN SUN

Slice that ripe green Avocado
Love it with my rice and beans
Oh it looks so ripe and yellow
Slice it like a Tangerine

Let's make love under La Palma
Lay out our blanket on the clean
Luqillo sand—allow the Puerto Rican
Sun to bath us with its warm Latino hands

Soothe our bodies, comfort our Souls
Heat our blood as we become one under
La Palma and Puerto Rican Sun

Jenny Terrero Rivera

SUBWAY TO MANHATTAN

Let's ride that A train
fast—so fast as we stand outside
between cars eating our salty white
pumpkin seeds—licking our lips,
keeping our balance—don't want
to fall between the cars and end up
underneath those rusted iron wheels.

Let's ride the train,
check out the Big Apple's
white-collar class with their
three-piece suits - ties - briefcases,
and up close to you, touching your
behind as Vietnam vets beg for a
quarter or a dime

The bums sleep taking up seats
with their smelly selves,
Elija Mohammed is selling his
propaganda: white man is the
the devil crap—maybe he is,
maybe he's not

And so—and so—lights blinking
on and off. The train like a fire-
breathing Dragon with a mighty roar,
rocks us back and forth, side to side,
slithers and slides as we ride leaving all
behind, speeding through those endless,
underground deep dark death tunnels

And we laugh, standing outside between
cars—the J to E.N.Y. Broadway

Junction, the Express to 34th Street,
skipping school, hoping we don't fall,
not caring at all. Looking forward to
those hot salty Manhattan pretzels.

MI FAMILIA

Get off your pity pot before
your ass gets too heavy,
my brother of color
my sister of color
my recovering familia

It's time to proclaim our
freedom from the man -
addictions - demons -
ourselves - and live!

We are slaves no more
servants to neither man nor
vices! For we have made a
conscious choice to live free
of chains just for today!

Jenny Terrero Rivera

OPRAH—IS THE MAN

I know your soul Oprah
just like mine—it took a lot of
strength for us to survive

You've moved ahead—conquered
your foes, trimmed and tossed out
your pain, yes—you told!

On TV for the world to know
Oprah a survivor - true
woman of soul.

You do your thing
live your life—speak your mind
you don't need to be Stedmen's wife!

Once free—we stay free
never more a prisoner to be!
Be a strong voice, my friend
for women like me!

That's right OPRAH—YOU THE MAN!
A woman of color—a woman of class
your spirit survived—your heart and your soul
conquering your demons—taking control!

You go, girl! You go!

FREDDIE PRINZE

Hey Mr. Prinze—you were the man
out of the ghetto right to the top
with your Chevy and pom-poms and the
dog whose head bobs up and down,
staring out at me from the rear
backseat window.

Yo, Mr. Man, on prime-time TV
the only Latino with his own show
who perform a comedy skit for the
president of the U.S. OF A.!

We were proud of you—our brown
brother but you blew it all up your nose
white Lady Love controlling your green,
out of your mind, forgetting your dream!

Your dream came too fast to see
Your fame too easy to be appreciated
Your responsibility too heavy to carry.

So you blew it all away, mi hermano,
with a gun to your head. My Latino
brother, you blew away your life and
our hope and faith in dreams.

Jenny Terrero Rivera

CAFE CON GALLETA

A mi me gusta
cafe con galleta,
Royal Lunch or
Unsalted Saltines

I like to dunk them
My sister likes to crush them
until they overflow her cup
not me

A mi me gusta
mi cafe con galleta
dulce, "sweet," con
leche sin nata

My coffee and crackers
you know what I mean
cafe con galleta
is breakfast for me.

lines-1 &2-I like coffee and crackers
lines-11 &12- sweet with milk and not that skin that floats on top when the milk is boiled

LA SISTEMA

Ya estoy cansado I am so tired
with the man and his control.
got busted and sentenced,
treatment or the hole

In this white man's rehab
I don't need to be
no way he gonna
control my destiny

Yo sé — yo soy el humbre I know - I am the man
yo puedo vencer I can beat this
I don't need your halfway
house or after-care plan.

I sell to vivir — I use, ¿y que? To live so what
mi vida es mía, can't you understand?
So get off my back
almighty white man!

line-1- I am tired lines-9&10-I know, I am, I can overcome
lines -13 &14-live- so what, my life is mine

Jenny Terrero Rivera

EL ALCOHOL

Mi amigo — Alcohol, my friend alcohol
me quita el dolor, takes away the pain
dolor profundo profound pain
en mi corazón in my heart
y en mi cuerpo, and my body

Amigo, penetra mis huesos, penetrate my bones
fluye en mis sangre. flow in my blood
Quiero poner mi labios sobre su boca
I want to place my lips, over your mouth
and drink of your dreams tomar de sus sueños
Quiero sentirte corriendo por mis
I want to feel you inside
entrañas, tocando cada herida, touching my wounds
abrazando mi soledad, embracing my loneliness

Sóbame, quita mi dolor, levanta caress me, take away
mi espíritu caído. Oh, amigo mio my pain, raise up my
spirit ¿en qué poner fé? Si no hay nadie in what shall I
have faith ni nada - solo tú, maldito Alcohol! in nothing
only you cursed alcohol

DESPAIR

surrounded by death
under big city lights
in this land of opportunity
there are many ways to die

am i cursed - am i damned
by a past witches brew
so much death around me
let me die too

funeral after funeral
we bury our blood
our children die of abuse
our teens by guns
our elders of Aids
drinking and drugs

under big city lights
in this land of opportunity
there are many ways to die
as a young black brother
I await my time

Jenny Terrero Rivera

HERITAGE

Let me seek out
and discover my heritage
allow my blood to turn
back the hands of time
a fine red line leading to
the simple life of family
and respect, children singing
in a language I no longer understand

The elders gather around the
burning sacrifice reading the
words in the smoke that
flows up into the air
spelling peace, tranquillity,
among tall bush trees
wild animals and Honey bees

Let us paint our faces and
share the pipe - let us dance
before our GOD in ritual
thanksgiving, for we are
glad - HE lives among us
a people so unknown
so simple - so innocent
so yesterday

CHOCOLATE MAN

baby man
chocolate candy man

sweet is you taste
upon my hot lips

dark - your skin
next to mine

you are my
chocolate candy man

come sweet thing
melt in my hands

mama and papa
would disagree

your dark skin
underneath me

but i don't care
what they believe

chocolate man
so right for me

Jenny Terrero Rivera

NEW YORK -A HELL OF A TOWN

madison and 86
come to mecca
14 street grenich village
bohemian - radicals
washington square park
steven Craig
edith
eugene
edgar's raven flies high
ebberts field, brooklyn dodgers
whip the butts off the yanks
broadway and 26 th.
the best theater
in the world
cole porter
lrving berlin
rogers and hemmestein
death of a sales men
south pacific
and a street car named desire
racial strife - protest
disco music
and serial killer
SON OF SAM

MY MOTHER'S PILON

Still useful and inviting as ever
familia gathers en el dia del Pabo on thanksgiving
Christmas, New Years
The Pilon would make it's appearance

Garlic cloves, green and red peppers
aji y recow, onions that burned my eyes
and thus the pounding begins
My Mothers Pilon I hold dear to my heart

As far back as I can remember
she would let me pound garlic
I could never grind it the way Mamma
would, but I loved to help her

Now that she is gone to the Father
I find myself filled with wonderful
memories every time I pull out
my mothers Pilon

It's aromas would flood the air
all my senses are pulled into
my mothers cozina kitchen
and I'd stop pounding,

she would be right beside me
I could hear her laugh
between her words
"Un poquito mas, Negrita" a little while more

Anyone looking at that Pilon would say,
wow that's old and worthless,
but, oh the value in every tiny crack
of my mothers Pilon!

JESUCRIS

PIRAGUA MAN

Raspar ese hielo
That cold brick of ice
Raspar ese hielo
Crystal clear and light

Raspar ese hielo
Dame una de pina
y una de coco
Piragua man
I like the way it taste

So cool and refreshing
On a hot New York City
summer day

line-1- scrape that block of ice
line-6 & 7 - give me one of pineapple and one coconut

Jenny Terrero Rivera

The following poems were added after the terrible tragedy in New York City
entitled -

A TRIBUTE TO MY HOME TOWN AND MY MULTICULTURAL BROTHERS AND SISTERS

INFINITE JUSTICE

Infinite Justice cried out the king
tears in his eyes
flaming swords—his wings

Righteous anger! Righteous anger!
Oh Lord my bowels will burst
Words of blood drip from the sky
Be strong! Be strong!
For us survive!

Iron, steel, blood soaked dust
Wall of many faces
Starring back at us
My GOD! My GOD!
In GOD we trust

The blow that struck to kill to crush
Yet stand, we stand, stronger, we must!
Not you not I, we will not die
For words of blood shout from the sky!
Stand strong! stand strong!
You must survive!

Jenny Terrero Rivera

RESURRECTED

Americans have been inspired
by all who gave up their lives
Priest, firemen, civilian
who did all to save a life

Patriotism, buried and dead
Resurrected from its dusty bed

Onward Christian soldier
fear not as you march on
fight for liberty, freedom, democracy
until the battles won!

Look up, look up and talk to GOD
He will help you stand
For if the enemy destroys your body
Your soul is in HIS hands!

I WANT TO KNOW WHY

Our Father who art in heaven
why didn't you do something?

My child, my child, I did, I did

Oh Father in heaven,
what did you do?

I sent my Holy Spirit
to warn people like you
my Angels I sent to pastors and priest
but man turns a deaf ear - refusing to believe

My Father my Father,
so many have died

Believe me my son, I also cried

blamed for the evil by the father of lies
he loves to destroy, steal and to kill
I offer life eternal on my holy hill

My Father, my Father
now what should we do

Allow me to heal you, hold you, love you
make you brand new!

ABOUT THE AUTHOR

I am the fourth child born to Puerto Rican parents living on the lower east side of Manhattan. I was raised in Brooklyn and began to write poetry and short stories in my preteens. By the time I was fourteen I was already drinking alcohol and experimenting with drugs. After the death of my husband, due to drugs, I sought help and recovery for my emotional problems and my addictions. I became an addiction counselor, educator and minister two years after treatment and worked in an inpatient facility for people in recovery and implemented a recovery program for my home church.

I have been working on my memoirs now for a number of years which will possibly be completed in another year. However, my collection of survival poetry entitled, "Tainted Soul," will follow the publication of "The Apple." "Tainted Soul," is a collection of poems I wrote during my years in treatment and is filled with a great deal of anger and the arguments I had with GOD.

Although my wish was to have "Tainted Soul" published first, I am proud to release "The Apple". Why? because I had lived a life of depression and deep emotional pain which you will clearly see in "Tainted Soul." I had always believed I was incapable of writing anything humorist and was quite surprised when I began to give birth to "The Apple." The poems in "The Apple" are events and personal experiences of my life, my culture and my environment while growing up. I had discovered that in the mist of great pain there was also humor, good memories and joy that I could not see before treatment. That is way I am so proud of this collection and happy that it's the first among my work to be published. It is not intended to offend anyone.

So I hope you enjoy it and remember to look for my other books.

www.ingramcontent.com/pod-product-compliance
Lightning Source LLC
Chambersburg PA
CBHW031316060726
47590CB00003B/1229